Napkin Folding & Place Cards for Festive Tables

Hans Tapper & Helena York

 Sterling Publishing Co., Inc. New York

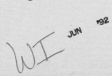

Photos: Photo-Design-Studio Gerhard Burock, Wiesbaden-Neurod

At this time, we would like to thank the following for their contributions:
H. and A. Wegener, Wiesbaden: Place cards made from dough
R. Strobel-Schulze, Taunusstein: Colorful flowers and nature scenes

Advice and directions given in this book have been carefully checked, prior to printing, by the Author and the Publisher. Nevertheless no guarantee can be given as to the outcome of projects and no responsibility taken for any eventual damage to persons and/or property.

Library of Congress Cataloging-in-Publication Data

Napkin folding & place cards for festive tables / Hans Tapper, Helena
   York ; [translated by Elizabeth Reinersmann].
         p.   cm.
      Translation of: Servietten dekorativ falten / H. Tapper and
   Tischkarten dekorativ gestalten / H. York.
      Includes index.
      ISBN 0-8069-5792-1
      1. Napkin folding.   2. Place cards.   I. Tapper, Hans.   Servietten
   dekorativ falten.   English.   1989.   II. York, Helena.   Tischkarten
   dekorativ gestalten.   English.   1989.   III. Title: Napkin folding
   and place cards for festive tables.
   TX879.N37   1989
   642'.7—dc20   89-4574
                                                              CIP

Translated by Elizabeth Reinersmann
English translation copyright © 1989 by Sterling Publishing Co., Inc.
387 Park Avenue South, New York, N.Y. 10016
Originally published under the titles, "Servietten dekorativ
falten" and "Tischkarten dekorativ gestalten" © 1986/1988
and 1988, respectively, by Falken-Verlag GmbH, 6272
Niederhausen/Ts., West Germany
Distributed in Canada by Sterling Publishing .
℅ Canadian Manda Group, P.O. Box 920, Station U
Toronto, Ontario, Canada M8Z 5P9
Distributed in Great Britain and Europe by Cassell PLC
Artillery House, Artillery Row, London SW1P 1RT, England
Distributed in Australia by Capricorn Ltd.
P.O. Box 665, Lane Cove, NSW 2066
Printed and bound in Hong Kong
All rights reserved
Sterling ISBN 0-8069-5792-1 Paper

Contents

The Art of Setting a Table

Many of us, at dinner parties, have looked with admiration, mixed, perhaps, with a little envy, at a wonderfully decorated table. Everything was just right; everything sparkled. The china, the silver and glassware, the candles and the flower arrangement were in exquisite taste. And last but not least, the intricately folded napkins and the artfully decorated place cards seemed to provide the final and perfect touches. Here is your opportunity to join the ranks of those party givers you have admired in the past.

The first part introduces you to the art of folding a napkin. Using napkins made out of cloth or paper, you will be able to achieve a napkin that will complement a brunch table with a rustic theme or create a sophisticated one perfect for any elegant dinner party.

The second part of the book introduces the card. We believe that no table decoration is complete unless it includes a place card at each setting. Your guests will not fail to notice with what care and thought you have prepared for their visit and you will get great satisfaction from your ability to express your aesthetic sense.

In both parts, we start with the basics and proceed to the elaborate. Before long, you will find yourself capable of producing table settings that are perfect for every occasion.

NAPKIN FOLDING

Introduction

Napkins, made from either fabric or paper, and folded decoratively, are necessities when it comes to setting a beautiful table. Those who object to the fancy folding of napkins seem to be concerned with the additional handling of the napkin, feeling that this might be unhygienic. But, a festive table that displays fine china and silverware and beautiful flowers is incomplete without an artfully folded napkin.

We know that the napkin, often of fine fabric, has been in use in Europe since the 15th century. They were first used at court dinner tables as a practical means of cleansing one's hands and mouth. They were often kept near the oven so that they could be brought to the table while still warm and were sometimes sprinkled with perfume.

Early in the 19th century the napkin became fashionable in less aristocratic circles. Paintings of people dining frequently show them with napkins tied around their necks for protection of their clothing.

Today, we put unfolded napkins on our laps and use them only to wipe our mouths during the course of a meal.

The classic napkin is of the same material as the tablecloth, usually cotton damask. Today, many different materials are used, including man-made fibres. Although there is a preference for napkins made from either cotton or linen mixtures, almost any napkin can be transformed into a wonderful creation.

A note of importance: whatever the fibre, the napkins should be slightly starched.

The quality—and price—of the different materials available, of course, varies. Just be sure that the material is not too thin; your creations won't hold up if it is.

Of course, paper napkins are suitable, but again, avoid the very inexpensive napkins. They do not lend themselves well to being folded.

Sizes of napkins vary. Those made from fabric are usually about 20 inches square (50 cm). But do not be concerned if the napkin is smaller. The folding techniques described in this book work well no matter what the size of the napkin.

Paper napkins are usually about 13 inches (33 cm) in size, or smaller. Again, except for the really small sizes, all folding methods can be used.

Note: Make sure that the napkins, regardless of size and material, are square.

Of course, you cannot use pins or glue. If you make sure that the napkin is without wrinkles and that your folds are exact and the creases sharp, you will be successful.

Have fun with your projects.

Pockets

Pocket 1

1. Position the smooth napkin in front of you, wrong side up.

4. Fold the top fold down as shown.

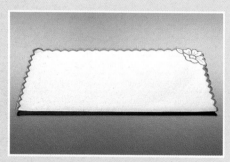

2. Fold upwards in the middle.

5. Take the second fold down also and tuck under the first fold.
This is one version of a "pocket."

3. Fold again to create a square, with open sides to the right and the top.

Pocket 2

1–3. Steps 1 to 3 are the same as for pocket 1;

4. Here, you tuck the first fold under to create a pocket.

Pocket 3

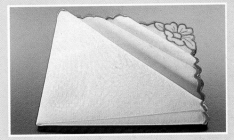

1–4. Steps 1 to 4 are the same as for pocket 2.

5. Tuck the first, the second and the third folds under, as shown (don't crease!), and you have 2 pockets.

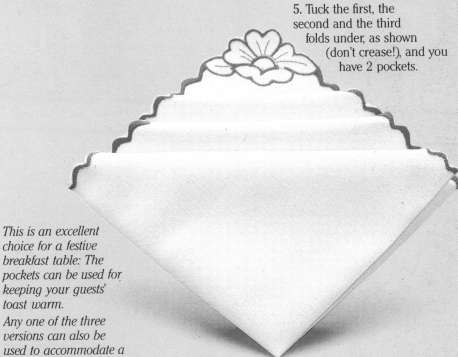

This is an excellent choice for a festive breakfast table: The pockets can be used for keeping your guests' toast warm.

Any one of the three versions can also be used to accommodate a menu.

Waves

Single Wave

1. Position your napkin in front of you, wrong side up.

3. Roll the left side towards the middle as shown; turn the napkin and you have a special place for a party favor.

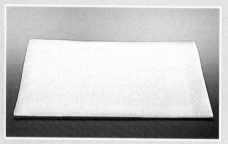

2. Fold in the middle, upwards.

Double Wave

1–3. Follow steps 1 through 3, as shown above.

4. Turn the right side under as shown.

5. This is what the double wave looks like.

Here is an example of the triple wave.

Triple Wave

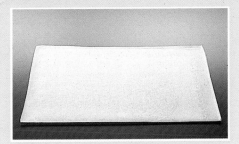

Steps 1 and 2 are the same as in the single wave.

3. Turn right side under first.

4. Lift napkin slightly in the middle, as shown, and fold against the right "wave."

5. Now roll the left side over and fold against the second "wave."

Lily

1. Position the napkin with the corners pointing up/down, left/right, respectively.

2. Fold the upper corner down, folding napkin in the middle.

3. Fold left and right corners down until sides meet in the middle.

4. Take both corners and fold up to the center point, as shown.

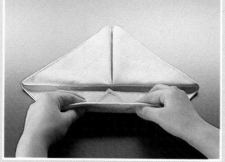

5. Take lower point, fold once to touch in the center of midline; fold again so that lower crease touches the midline, as in picture.

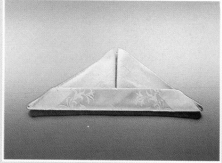

6. Once again, fold this portion upwards and over the midline.

7. Take napkin on both sides and insert right corner into left.

8. Set napkin down and pull the two outer folds gently down and tuck into the fold as shown.

11

Pointed Hat

1. Position napkin, wrong side up.

4. Turn your hands towards the middle, forming a cone.

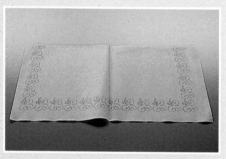

2. Fold napkin down at the middle.

5. Fold right portion of napkin over the cone so that both corners meet.

3. Hold the upper left corner between thumb and index finger, as shown, and gently fold the material.

6. Together, they can be then folded and creased.

The "Pointed Hat" is ideal for a table set for a rustic brunch. This folding method works very well with a paper napkin.

Cap and Variations

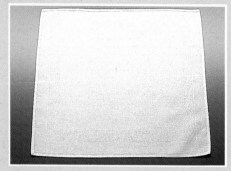

1. Position napkin in front of you, wrong side up.

4. Fold the lower corner of the square up by about one fourth.

2. Fold up at the middle.

5. Insert the right corner into the left.

3. Fold again, to the right, at the middle.

6. This is your cap.

Version 1

7. Gently pull down the point of the triangle.

Version 2

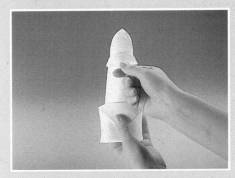

8. Pull down the first fold of the top "leaf."

Bishop's Mitre

1. Position napkin on table with wrong side up.

2. Fold up at the middle.

3. Pull upper left corner down to the middle.

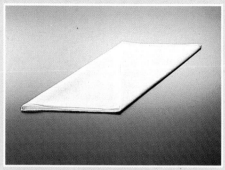

4. With the lower right corner up, fold the napkin into a rhombus shape.

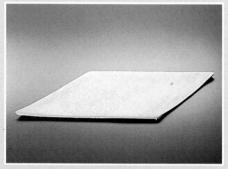

5. Turn your "rhombus" over.

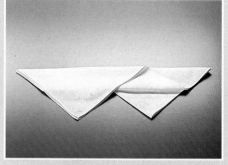

6. Fold lengthwise, letting the corners extend as shown.

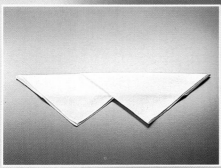

7. Unfold right triangle, turn napkin over (from left to right) and fold triangle down over the edge.

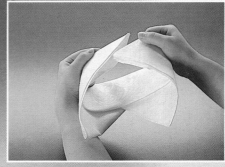

8. Turn napkin, again from left to right, and insert right corners into the left, as shown.

Fluted Crests

Multi-Fluted Crest

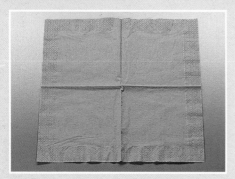

1. Position napkin in front of you.

4. Fold the right corner of the triangle to the left.

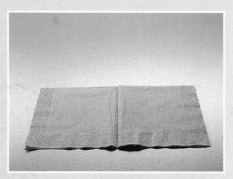

2. Fold down at the middle.

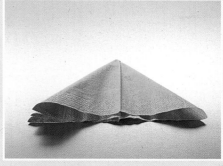

5. Pull the right lower corner of top layer to the left corner.

3. Pull lower corner of the top layer over to the right corner, forming a triangle.

6. Fold the right half of triangle over to the left and sharply crease the napkin at that edge. Pull the napkin up at the tip and set it on the fluted points.

This is the finished multi-fluted crest. This design can be used with paper napkins, but if you do so, be careful when folding the triangles. Crease only the very last fold.

Double-Fluted Crest

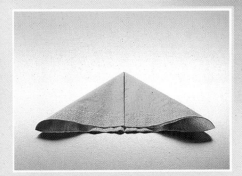

Fold as in steps 1 and 2 of first crest.

1. Pull the upper left and right corner down to the middle.

2. Pull napkin up at the tip and set it on the fluted points.

Fans

Single Fan

1. Position napkin in front of you, wrong side facing up.

2. Fold lower edge up at the middle.

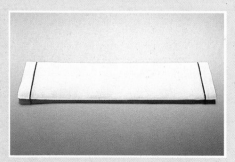

3. Fold in half and turn 90 degrees.

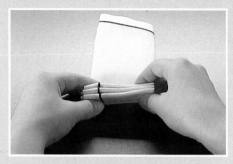

4. Fold this rectangle, harmonica-fashion, as shown, starting from the narrow side.

5. Press folded napkin together as shown.

6. Hold lower edge in one hand and pull upper edges to the left and right, respectively.

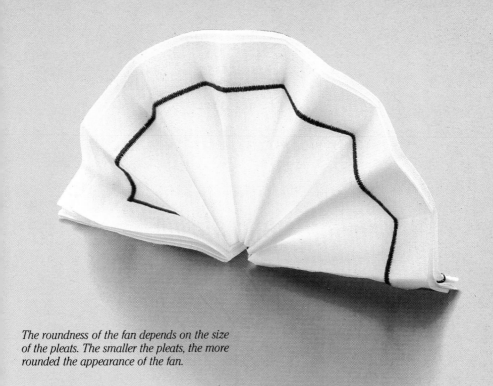

The roundness of the fan depends on the size of the pleats. The smaller the pleats, the more rounded the appearance of the fan.

Double Fan

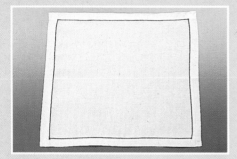

1. Position the napkin on table with wrong side up.

4. Fold napkin, harmonica-style, starting at the small side.

2. Fold from lower edge up at the middle.

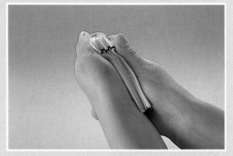

5. Press napkin together and hold folds tightly in your left hand.

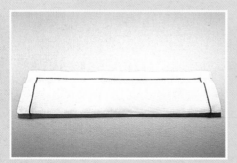

3. Fold rectangle up at lower edge by one third.

6. Pull out small folds as shown, one by one.

Note: After every pull, press the napkin tightly together again.

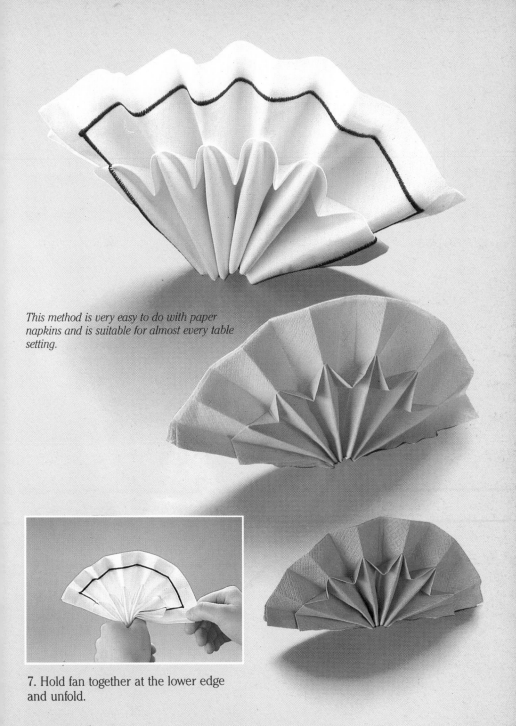

This method is very easy to do with paper napkins and is suitable for almost every table setting.

7. Hold fan together at the lower edge and unfold.

Cresting Fan

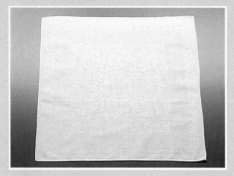

1. Position napkin, wrong side facing up, in front of you.

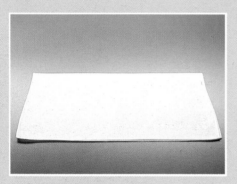

2. Fold down at the middle.

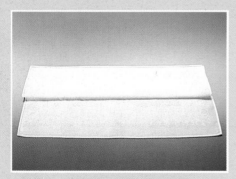

3. Fold top layer up from the middle; turn napkin to the other side from left to right.

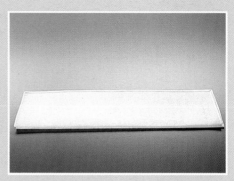

4. Fold lower portion up at the middle.

5. Fold rectangle, harmonica-fashion, starting at the small side.

6. Press napkin together tightly and hold it, with the open edge pointing down, in your left hand.

This elegant and graceful decoration is perfect for a formal table setting.

7. Pull the inside of each fold to the outside, pressing folds together again after each pull.

8. Unfold the fan as shown.

Standing Fan

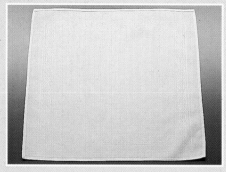

1. Position the napkin in front of you, wrong side facing up.

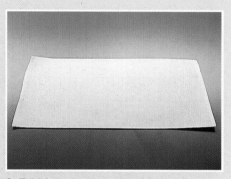

2. Fold lower edge up at the middle.

3. Turn the napkin, with the short side facing you, and fold it, harmonica-fashion, in even pleats. Press creases sharply. One third of the napkin remains unfolded.

4. Turn the napkin over, with the unfolded portion pointing to your right.

5. Fold the pleated portion at the middle, as shown.

6. Fold the unpleated portion of the napkin diagonally down.

The fan will stand securely due to the smooth base.

7. The portion that extends beyond the fold is turned under and will serve as the base.

8. Put the fan on its base; it will unfold by itself.

A Tulip—and a Variation
(also called Banana or Ear-of-Corn)

1. Position an unwrinkled napkin on the table, with one corner pointing towards you.

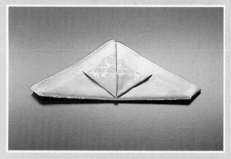

4. Now fold the lower portion upwards (positioning the tip a few centimetres below the top point) and the tip back down again, as shown.

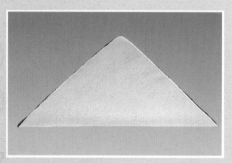

2. Fold the lower point up to form a triangle.

5. Insert the right corner inside the left.

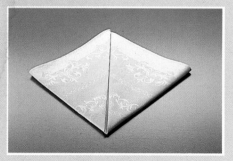

3. Fold both lower corners towards the middle to form a square.

6. Pull down the ends of the two top layers, as shown.

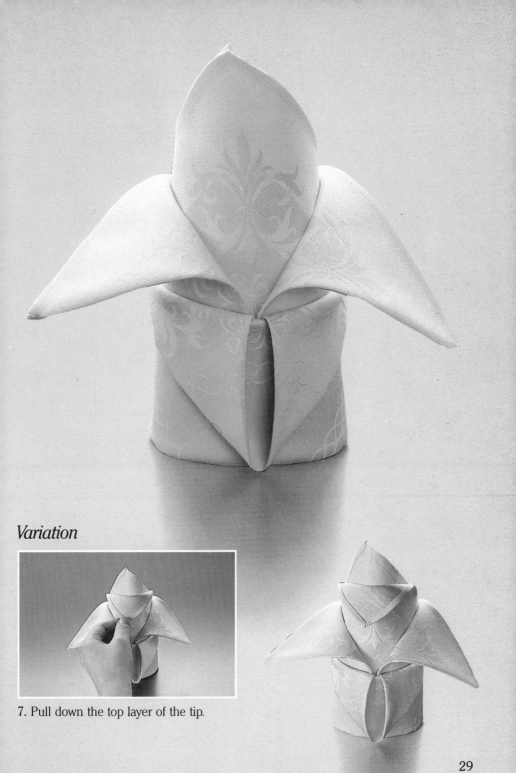

Variation

7. Pull down the top layer of the tip.

Lady's-Slipper Orchid

1. Position the napkin on the table with the wrong side facing up.

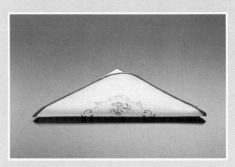

4. Fold the square into a triangle with the open sides on top.

2. Fold napkin up at the middle.

5. Fold the left and right sides of the triangle so that they touch in the middle.

3. Fold napkin in half from left to right, to form a square.

6. Fold the tips that are extending beyond the lower edge under and together. This is the back of the "slipper," which you hold together tightly in your left hand.

This decoration also looks attractive if the size of the napkin is larger and the fabric somewhat heavier than usual.

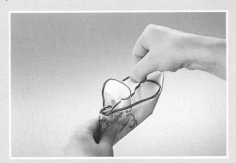

7. Continue to hold tightly, as you pull out the individual "leaves."

Artichoke

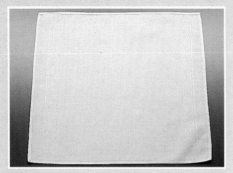

1. Position the napkin in front of you, wrong side facing up.

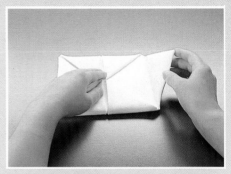

4. Again, fold all four corners into the middle, supporting the center.

2. Fold all four corners inside, meeting in the center.

5. Carefully pull out the tips that are hidden behind each corner, always supporting the napkin in the center.

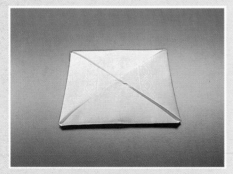

3. Repeat: Fold all four corners to the center; turn napkin over to the other side.

6. It is easy now to pull the corners up and shape the "Artichoke."

The "Artichoke" is a very useful addition to your table decorations, since the center accommodates small plates or small (crystal) bowls.

Variation

7. Pull out the remaining tips that a hidden.

A Bouquet

1. Place two thin paper napkins diagonally on top of each other.

2. Lift both napkins in the center and shake gently.

3. After pressing the tips together, insert them into a wine glass.

Special effects can be achieved if the napkins are of different and contrasting colors.

PLACE-CARD MAKING

As discussed, place cards are of great importance when it comes to decorating a festive table. After you have practised the basic steps, you will find that the possibilities and choices of how to decorate them seem endless.

You might wish to color-coordinate the cards to match your table setting, or you might want to create a contrast. You might consider decorating the cards with the symbols of your guests' professions, favorite sports, hobbies or astrological signs. Of course, an obvious decoration is to display the theme of the party: the celebration of a wedding or anniversary, a birthday, a graduation, and so forth.

Some people hesitate to prearrange their guests' seating order. They are unsure as to who wants to sit with whom. If this is the case, we suggest that you prepare your cards and place them in a pretty basket. As your guests enter the dining room, they pick up their cards and choose where they wish to sit.

Another way to do it is to ask your guests to be seated and then add the respective cards to their place settings.

After the decision to make your own cards, decide on the size of the cards and the material you wish to use. We preferred to stay almost exclusively with the square format. But for the adventurous, we have included several ideas to try. For example, if you are a nature lover you might gather a few leaves and/or flowers (dried flowers in the wintertime) along with some bark and surprise your friends with the truly unusual.

Use your imagination and create your own cards, using this array of samples as inspiration. You will find that there is no limit to your creativity.

But whatever designs you choose, we hope that you will enjoy yourself creating them and that your family, your friends, and your colleagues will be surprised and impressed by your artistry.

Material

Following is a list of the materials you will need for your projects.

For the card itself a stiff paper or cardboard (stationery shops carry what you need: poster board, construction paper, photo album pages, index cards, laminated gift cartons and the like)

soft pencil (#2) and pencil sharpener

ruler, 6 inches long, preferably with a metal edge

triangle

utility knife*

scissors

rubber cement

transparent tape

assortment of soft-tipped pens and crayons

assortment of letters and numbers in different sizes and with an adhesive backing

*Be very careful with this tool when children are present, especially when they are working with you.

Note: Each sample in the book lists all of the materials that are needed for that particular project.

37

Basic Technique

Material: carton or stiff paper, pencil, ruler, utility knife, and soft-tipped pen

1. Cut a piece of carton into a square, measuring 3½ inches (8 cm).

4. Fold card along the crease.

2. Mark middle with pencil.

5. Flatten card to decorate.

3. With the ruler at the metal edge, crease along the pencil line with the utility knife, taking care that it makes a crease, not a cut.

There are, of course, many ways to write the name on a card: with a soft-tipped pen, with crayons, using ready-made letters from the stationery store or cutting them out from a magazine, making a "letter-salad" out of it all, in the same or in different colors! You "name it"; the choice is yours.

Press-on Letters

1. Make a thin pencil line ⅛ inch (3 mm) below the line on which you want your printed name to "rest."

3. Hold the sheet securely in place and press the letter with a wooden stick.

2. Transfer the letters to the card by placing the line that is under the respective letter directly on the pencil line.

4. After completion of the name, cover the card with a thin piece of paper and rub over the whole name to ensure that the letters are all securely attached to the card. Erase the pencil line.

Ribbon Decoration

Material: gift-wrap ribbon.

1. Proceed with the basic technique.

3. Curl the ribbons over the sharp edge of a scissor blade and fasten to card.

2. Cut ribbon in 8-inch (20-cm) lengths and combine into a small bouquet.

4. Unfold card, print name, and refold on crease line.

Yarn Decoration

Material: wool yarn

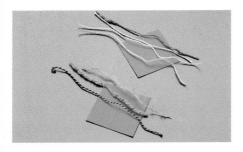

1. Choose and cut your yarn in 5-inch (12.7-cm) lengths.

2. Attach yarn to card with rubber cement, as shown.

3. Print and fold card on crease.

Gift-Wrap Paper Decoration

Material: gift-wrap paper. . . .

1. Prepare card according to instructions on page 38. Cut triangles or strips from the paper.

2. Attach gift-wrap paper with rubber cement to card (making sure that enough room is left to write name). Print name and fold card on crease.

Or Feathers

Material: feathers

1. Prepare card as before, attach glue to feather and position on card. Print name and fold card on crease.

2. If you use a large enough feather, it is possible to punch a small hole approximately 2 centimetres from the outer lower edge. Pull feather through hole and secure in the back with transparent tape, as shown.

Decoration with a Fan

Material: gift-wrap paper

1. Prepare place card (see page 38).

3. Fold paper, accordion-fashion, in approximately ¼-inch (6-mm) folds.

2. Choose the shape of the fan and cut paper accordingly (measurements for the other shapes are given with the instructions).

4. Shape into either a fan, a circle or a wedge; glue to card, print name and fold card on crease.

The following are examples of different shapes.

Anne

Anne:

Cut a square of approximately 4 inches (10 cm) diagonally and fold the triangle accordion-fashion. Glue thicker portion together and attach it to the card as shown.

Soraya:

A strip of paper approximately 1¾ × 5½ inches (4 × 14 cm) is folded accordion-fashion, beginning at the narrow end. Fold in half, glue halves together, unfold fan after glue has dried, and attach base of fan to card, print name and fold at crease.

Ellen:

Cut a strip of paper approximately 1¾ × 5½ inches (4 × 14 cm) and fold, starting from the narrow side; glue the folds together a little over ½ inch (about 1.5 cm) as shown, to create a stem. Bend stem to one side, unfold fan and attach to card.

Nadine:

Cut a strip of paper approximately 3½ × 4 inches (8 × 10 cm) and fold accordion-fashion, starting at the wide side. Glue accordion folds together from about the middle of the fan, creating a stem, unfold fan and attach to card.

Melanie:

Fold paper accordion-fashion, starting at the small side, from a strip of paper approximately 1 × 8 inches (2.5 × 20 cm). Cut a toothpick in half and attach to the respective last folds. Unfold fan ¾ of the way and glue toothpicks to card as shown.

Paper Flowers

Material: round coasters for cups or glasses or round 1-cup coffee filters.

1. Prepare card with the 3¼ inch (8 cm) measurements given on page 38. Consider a larger card for the fluffier double flower.

3. Crease round coaster several times in half as shown.

2. With utility knife cut a triangle in lower left corner of card, about ¾ inch (1.5 cm) from left and ⅞ inch (2 cm) from the lower edge.

Note: A hole, punched out with a hole-puncher, is also very practical.

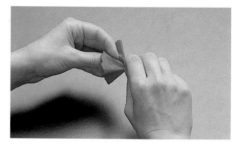

4. Fold paper together between four fingers as shown, and create a little stem by twisting the end; attach this single-blossom flower through hole to card.

5. For the double-blossom flower it is best to use paper coasters because they are made out of several layers.

Once the paper is folded and stem formed, pull the layers to the outside, starting at the innermost layer.

6. Push stem of your flower through hole, as shown, and secure in back with transparent tape.

Umbrella

Material: Round coasters for glasses and cups, toothpicks, small beads.

1. Prepare card (see page 38).

4. Reinforce the creases by pushing thumbnail along the edges.

2. Cut a small triangle or punch a small hole in the left or right corner, approximately ⅝ inch (1.5 cm) from the side and ⅞ inches (2 cm) from the lower edge.

5. Turn paper over, align two adjoining folds and crease the paper to create a reverse fold; this will make the umbrella folds.

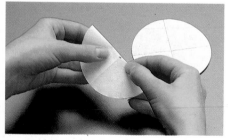

3. Crease paper in the middle, as shown, to create four equal quarters.

6. Turn umbrella around; apply a drop of glue in its center.

7. Flip umbrella over and press tip with glue onto a toothpick.

8. A small pearl bead attached to the tip of the umbrella secures the paper to the toothpick.

9. Push the end of the umbrella, as shown, through hole in card and secure on other side with transparent tape.

Palm Tree

Material: gift-wrap paper.

1. Prepare card (see page 38) and cut a small space that will accommodate the finished product.

3. With utility knife cut paper in equal ¼-inch (5-mm) strips, starting at the middle and cutting to the end.

2. Cut a strip of paper, measuring approximately 2½ × 4¾ inches (6 × 12 cm), from the wrapping paper.

4. Roll paper tightly, starting at the small, uncut end.

5. Starting from the outside, take each individual strip and roll it over the end of a pencil; this will give the paper strips a palm-like appearance.

6. Push end of palm tree through the space on card and secure in back with transparent tape.

Rafael

Margarita

Little

Material: transparent paper, soft-tipped pen, #2 pencil, crayons, yarn.

1. Prepare your card (see page 38) but do *not* crease (with utility knife).

4. Position the transparent paper over the card on the pencil line, with the blackened side facing down, and a portion of the mouse extending above the midline.

2. Draw a small mouse, or transfer a ready-made outline of a mouse, on transparent paper.

5. Outline the shape of mouse with a hard pencil or pen.

3. On the reverse side, blacken the outline and surrounding area of the mouse by rubbing a pencil as shown.
52

6. Put the final touches on your drawing and/or color the mouse.

7. Now: *crease card*, as outlined in "basic techniques" on page 38, to the left and the right of your mouse, but do *not cut* through it.

8. Carefully *cut* that portion of the mouse that extends *above* the midline, as shown.

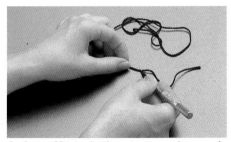

9. Cut a 3¾-inch (8-cm) piece of yarn of your choice for the tail and attach it to your mouse.

10. Print name and fold card in half at midline; the upper portion of your mouse will now extend beyond the top of the card.

Numbers

Material: transparent paper, soft-tipped
pen, pencil, crayons.

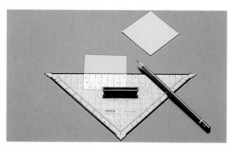

1. Prepare your card as outlined on page
38, but only mark your midline with
pencil; do *not* crease with knife.

2. Draw a straight line on the transparent
paper and transfer the numbers you wish
to use on that line.

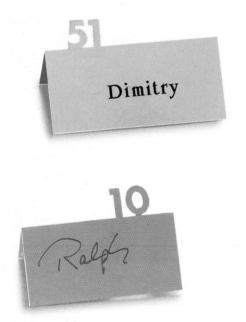

3. Blacken the reverse side of the transparent paper, covering the numbers and the surrounding area.

5. *Cut* numbers by outlining the outer contours with knife, except, of course, where they rest on the midline.

4. Position the line on transparent paper on top of the midline of your card, with numbers almost ⅝ inch (15 mm) away from the outside edge.

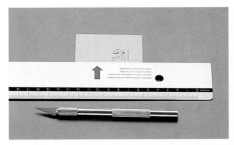

6. *Crease* midline of card at the right and left of the numbers.

7. Fold card in half, making sure that the cutting around the numbers is done cleanly. Print name (see also page 38–39).

A Party Hat

Material: photo album paper, confetti or small decorative stars, elastic yarn, cotton or feathers.

1. Cut a circle with a radius of a little over 9½ inches (24 cm) and divide in four equal sections.

4. Print name somewhere in the middle.

2. Shorten both straight lines (each from 12 cm or 4¾ inches in length) by ⅜–⅝-inch (1–1.6-cm), mark both lines ½ inch (1.2 cm) from the top and connect both points; cut.

5. For easier shaping, pull the carton over the edge of the table.

3. Make a pencil line along both straight lines, ¼ inch (6 mm) inside the edges; crease pencil lines with utility knife and bend both sides gently.

6. Glue both sides together along the ¼-inch (6-mm) crease.

7. Decorate hat with confetti or glitter, attaching either cotton, feathers, or ribbon-ringlets to the top.

8. Attach approximately 16–20 inches (40 to 50 cm) elastic yarn by making two small holes opposite each other about ⅜ inch (1 cm) from the edge.

Place Cards Made of Dough (nonedible)

Material: water colors, brush, soft-tipped pen, clear high-gloss or satin varnish.

Ingredients for the dough
17½ oz (500 g) flour
17½ oz (500 g) salt
1–2 tb. wallpaper paste
1–10 tb. liquid color—depending on how dark you intend the tint to be (leave out if you want to paint figures/shapes).
10 oz (300 ml) water

Mix dry ingredients, add water (and tint if desired) and work dough until smooth and not sticking to your fingers.

Note: If you use tint and would like different parts in different colors, you should wash your hands in between to ensure that the colors do not mix.

The drying process: This process is of special importance for the stability of the finished form.

1. Preheat oven to 125 °F (60 °C), put form in oven, with door left open, and predry dough for 12–15 hrs.

2. Close door, increase temperature to 300 °F (150 °C) and dry for another 3–5 hrs.

Check dough and fill any and all cracks or pores that develop during the drying process with thinned-out dough.

In order that the finished form does not absorb humidity from the air you must seal it with several coats of varnish, either high-gloss or satin finish.

Varnish is best absorbed when the form is still warm; therefore, return it to the oven repeatedly.

If you want your figures to stand on a base, make it separately. Dampen both pieces at the point of contact and join them together.

The figure and base shown on page 27, top row, was painted after the drying process; the dough therefore was left plain.

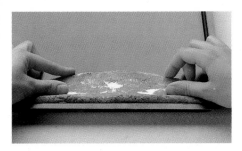

1. Form base for your figure, as shown.

2. Head, neck, arms, and feet are formed separately from strips and little balls of dough and joined before drying.

Flowers

Material: any small container that will accommodate the shell of an egg, eggs, dried flowers, florist's clay, and glue.

1. Empty the contents of an egg, wash and dry the inside. Attach some glue to the rim of the container you want to use and decorate with small leaves and flowers.

2. Print name on the eggshell and fill partially with florist's clay for the flower arrangement.

Nature Scene

Material: a piece of bark, small pieces of wood, dried leaves, flowers and fruits, shells, glue, felt pen.

1. Arrange the diverse items into a pretty bouquet and glue onto a piece of bark or wood.

2. Printing of the name can be done on a shell or leaf.

Stone

Material: stone

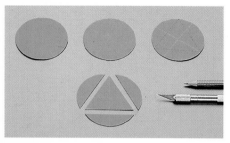

1. A stone, about 1½–2 inches (4–5 cm) in size, is scrubbed clean, attached to a piece of cardboard in the shape of a triangle, about 5–6 cm in size.

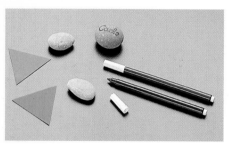

2. Print name on stone and glue to carton.

Easter Bunny

Material: carton, eggs, print-on faces of Easter bunnies.

1. Cut carton into strips, 2.5–4 cm × 12 cm. Print name. Shape strip into a ring; glue together.
Note: If you pull the carton, before gluing, over the edge of the table, it will be easy for the ring to be glued.

2. Hardboil eggs, attach faces and glue to the ring.

Index